Bible St

C000002825

7 Sessions for Homegroup
and Personal Use

Ruth

Loving Kindness in Action

Elizabeth Rundle

Published 2002 by CWR, Waverley Abbey House, Waverley Lane,
Farnham, Surrey GU9 8EP, England, UK.

See back of book for list of National Distributors.

Unless otherwise indicated, all Scripture references are from the Holy Bible:
New International Version (NIV), copyright © 1973, 1978, 1984 by the
International Bible Society.

Concept development, editing, design and production by CWR.
Front cover image: Roger Walker.
Printed by Linney Print.

ISBN 1-85345-231-9

Contents

Introduction

For a book of only four chapters, Ruth has a very prominent place in people's hearts. It is a story in the best riches-to-rags-to-riches mould, and we can well imagine it being told around the campfires in ancient Judea. However, it is far more than just a love story – the relationships it portrays become reflections of God's covenant relationship with His people.

It may have been written at the time of Ezra and Nehemiah or much earlier in the days of Solomon. It holds a significant place within Judaism as well, being the book read from the Torah at the festival of Shavuot, also known as Pentecost.

If there is one word to describe the lesson to be learnt from this short book, we could perhaps do no better than to use the word – trust.

The story touchingly illustrates total dependence on the providence of the one eternal and living God – the God of Israel. Ruth and her mother-in-law, Naomi, display a deep, uncomplicated trust in this God, who is their Creator, their Protector and Redeemer. We see the roots of this trust in the literature of the Psalms. For example:

He who dwells in the shelter of the Most High ...
will say of the Lord, "He is my refuge and my fortress,
  my God, in whom I trust." (Psalm 91:1–2)

They remembered that God was their Rock,
  that God Most High was their Redeemer. (Psalm 78:35)

Ruth is also a story of ordinary people living through trials and tribulations which speak across time and culture to us in our own generation. No charismatic leader to

praise, no crushing defeat of enemies to celebrate and no
theological insights to pass into posterity – none of these
things; yet this book is a gem. It brims with kindness,
loyalty, faith and timeless values which cement peoples
together.

The opening words give us the social and political
background. "In the days when the judges ruled ..." The
setting is that raw and brutal time when the different
clans were settling down to embryo nationhood prior to
the monarchy. Because they were without overall
leadership and "did evil in the eyes of the Lord and
served the Baals" (Judg. 2:11), the Lord God periodically
raised up certain "judges". It must have been frustrating
for these judges, as we read further on in chapter 2 verse
17, "they would not listen to their judges ..." and "when
the judge died, the people returned to ways even more
corrupt ..." (v.19). The tribes, settled into the promised
land, were easily tempted by the idol worship of their
neighbours, quickly falling under the influence of "other
gods", in particular the god Baal. Complacency and
disobedience to God's commands led to general religious
and moral decay which, in turn, led to unrest amongst
them and hostility towards foreign groups. The alarming
consequences of turning their hearts away from God,
written down to form Deuteronomy chapter 28,
conveniently slid from their conscience. It was every
man – and woman – for themselves.

It is against this fierce backdrop that we are introduced to
Elimelech's family whose central character is a daughter-
in-law he may or may not have known, Ruth. The whole
beginning is shrouded in conjecture. Why was there such
a severe famine around the fertile area of Bethlehem? Was
it caused by direct neglect because the men were away
from the land, skirmishing? Furthermore, Moab was not
exactly flavour of the month; it had, in the time of the
judges, conquered Jericho (Judg. 3:13) and ruled the

Israelites for eighteen years (v.14). And, because the Moabites had been distinctly unfriendly when the Israelites came out of Egypt, no Moabite was allowed to "enter the assembly of the Lord" (see Deut. 23:3).

We need all our powers of imagination to understand the immense significance of Ruth being a Moabite. How would the story have been accepted in the days when Ezra and Nehemiah were doing all they could to prohibit mixed marriages? Perhaps the author wrote Ruth to counteract those rigorous decrees. And what would have been the reaction of the people to know that their revered King David's grandmother was a foreigner?

I love to think of Jesus hearing this story. The implications here are gloriously inclusive, as we shall see in Week 7. The Messiah, our Saviour, is the Saviour for every individual from every nation.

We have already mentioned the great themes of kindness, loyalty and faith in the book of Ruth and these stand alongside fundamental issues which still affect people every day. Poverty, bereavement, childlessness, racial tension and human rights.

With the benefit of hindsight, we are able to look at the teachings of Jesus and realise His own compassion for the alienated and vulnerable in society. In this book we find an uncomfortable challenge to ourselves, our own faith and values and how we witness to our Christianity in daily life.

May our study of Ruth inspire and motivate us into deeper faith, visionary hope and steadfast love. In the words of an old hymn:

We'll praise him for all that is past,
And trust him for all that's to come.

WEEK 1

Disaster

Opening Icebreaker

Everyone put a map pin onto a world map to mark your country of birth, also marking where you now live, if different. Then each say two sentences about yourselves.

Bible Readings

- Ruth 1:1–5; 19–21
- Leviticus 19:1–9
- Deuteronomy 7:1–4
- Judges 2:11–17
- Lamentations 1:1–2

Opening Our Eyes

Throughout history there have always been times of migration. Over the centuries economic crises have forced millions of people to migrate with dreams of a better land and prosperity. Perhaps we could think, for example, of the effects of the nineteenth-century potato famine in Ireland and the depressions that hit Scotland, Wales and Cornwall, forcing people to emigrate. Disasters are part and parcel of human history and great stories of courage, perseverence and, above all, hope, shine through dark and tragic episodes. Such is the story of Ruth.

The opening sentence is loaded with drama. These were the days before the rule of any king and the previous book, Judges, makes it perfectly plain that the people did virtually as they wanted. In any time of famine the unscrupulous take advantage while the poor – and honest – suffer. That a famine should take hold in Bethlehem underlines the severity of the situation, because the very name Bethlehem, Beit Lechem, means "house of bread". The writer may be suggesting that Elimelech found it impossible to survive in his home town because the famine also raised issues of principle. What is quite certain is that the famine was a life and death situation and Elimelech decided the only way to preserve the family was to take a drastic step and leave for another country.

A likely route from Bethlehem to Moab would be down through the Judean hills to cross the River Jordan at the top end of the Dead Sea. From there they would have travelled through the baking barren landscape before ending up some eighty miles from Bethlehem, in Moab. Today it is part of Jordan. As we read, we realise that Elimelech must have died very soon after their arrival in the land of Moab. This situation was a disaster for Naomi whose faith in the one true God of Israel precluded her from finding a Moabite husband (Ezra 10:2–5).

However, such thoughts did not deter her sons, Mahlon and Chilion, who both married lovely Moabite girls, Orpah and Ruth.

For "about ten years" Moab was home to Naomi, her sons and daughters-in-law. As the rest of the story unfolds it is obvious that both the girls had enormous fondness for their mother-in-law. Naomi's bereavement was eased by the new family life, but there also lurked a sadness that neither son produced an heir. For that time and culture it was imperative to have a son in order to continue the line and inheritance.

Names in the Bible held great significance. To know a person's name was to know something about them (for instance, Genesis 32:27–29). The name Mahlon appears to mean "to be sick" and his brother's name, Chilion, indicated one who was "pining" or "failing". Sadly, neither of the young men enjoyed robust health and, after some ten years in Moab, they both died.

The opening verses of Lamentations portray a vivid picture of biblical widowhood. Disaster hits Naomi once more. To lose her husband was trial enough, but to bury both her sons was devastating. In the loss of her sons Naomi lost her own security and place in the community. Remember how Deuteronomy lumps together "aliens and widows". She suddenly finds herself in a foreign land with no means of support. Poor Naomi feels the Lord has dealt her a harsh blow and in her despair we catch the murmur of our own questioning.

Discussion Starters

1. What similarities would you identify between our present-day attitudes and those found in the days when the judges ruled?

_____

_____

_____

_____

2. Why should Elimelech have chosen to travel to Moab instead of turning to more fertile regions towards the Mediterranean coast?

_____

_____

_____

_____

3. What circumstances today force people to leave their homes?

_____

_____

_____

_____

4. In what ways would Naomi have witnessed to her faith in Israel's God?

_____

_____

_____

_____

5. Ruth and Orpah were left childless. Do you think there is still a residue of unfair expectations upon young couples to have children?

_____

_____

_____

_____

6. In biblical times the widows were people at the bottom of society. In what ways do we think differently today?

_____

_____

_____

_____

7. Naomi felt the Lord had dealt harshly with her. How would you try to convince her that her situation was not a punishment from the Lord?

_____

_____

_____

_____

8. For what reasons have you been inclined to feel that God has dealt harshly with you or perhaps with a family member or friend?

_____

_____

_____

_____

Personal Application

There are a whole lot of issues here to which we can personally apply ourselves. The spectre of famine hangs over millions of God's children every day. We have a Christian obligation to acknowledge the needs of others and, by our own thoughtful stewardship of resources and our attitude to shopping (eg, where possible, Fairtrade, Traidcraft), we can demonstrate our commitment to a sharing of God's wonderful world. We might also examine our attitudes towards mothers-in-law and widowhood. Apart from social sympathy, do we really stop to think what the enormity of the situation means? The Church is full of widows, and mothers-in-law are not always a joke! God works His purpose through us to create a better community.

Seeing Jesus in the Scriptures

Our Saviour Jesus, who came to be the Saviour of the world, had an eye and a deep compassion for the lowly and the individual. At the beginning of chapter 21 of Luke's Gospel, Jesus publicly identifies a poor widow for giving to God a greater gift than any of the rich people around her. Also, His own mother, Mary, may have been a widow for several years. And in the Gospel of Mark chapter 1, the incident is recorded where Jesus heals Peter's mother-in-law (vv.29–31). Our Lord Jesus extends His hand to touch the afflicted and those on the edge of society. In the power of the Holy Spirit we, as Christians, seek to follow His example.

WEEK 2

Choices

Opening Icebreaker

Looking again at last week's world map, everyone add a pin in a country where either you have a friend or relative or in a place you would love to visit. This gives the opportunity for getting to know the group's links and again shows how many parts of the world are touched by such a small number of people.

Bible Readings

- Ruth 1:6–18
- Deuteronomy 30:15–19
- John 15:15–17
- 1 Corinthians 1:27

Opening Our Eyes

Life is full of decisions. Most are just our routine bits and bobs: of choosing between toast or cereal, deliberating on new colour schemes for the bedroom or deciding whether we go out and shop now or leave it till the rain clears up.

There are also those choices we make which are momentous and life-changing. The core twelve verses from Ruth this week speak to us of just those kind of decisions. Let's take a closer look at the picture.

Naomi, Ruth and Orpah are now three widows. In Old Testament times, wives were only possessions and had no rights of inheritance. Once widowed they were on their own. Naomi is far away from her homeland and culture and, as their mother-in-law, she is presumably much older than Ruth and Orpah. She sees no future for herself in Moab and when she hears that the famine is over in Bethlehem, she makes her decision to return home. Although Orpah loves her mother-in-law dearly and does not want to be parted from her, in the end she decides to stay with her own people. Ruth makes the mega choice. She not only determines to leave her own country and return to her late husband's home town where she will be a foreigner, but she also chooses to commit herself to Naomi and, more amazingly, to Naomi's God.

It is touching to read Naomi outlining the pointlessness of the girls staying with her. She can only see their future security in finding Moabite husbands and having children. She could offer them nothing. Naomi's prayer gives us a glimpse of the previously happy family unit: "The Lord deal kindly with you, as you have dealt with the dead, and with me" (NKJV). (This word *kindly*, keeps cropping up – "shows kindness" in NIV – and we shall explore it in Week 4.) We admire Naomi's selfless approach in being willing to lose the girls' companionship in order that they could begin life anew. It was a demonstration that she truly loved them that she was willing to give them their freedom.

Orpah, though devastated to say goodbye to both Ruth and Naomi, makes her choice to stay with her own people. Their parting is deeply sorrowful and sincere. They are true friends.

Ruth, on the other hand, remains with Naomi. Indeed, in verse 18, Naomi realises that she "was determined to go with her ...". In fact, Ruth had been converted! Such was Naomi's living and kind faith that Ruth willingly gave herself to the mercy of the God of Israel. She had witnessed the obvious trust that Naomi placed in the providence and guidance of her God and it so motivated and inspired Ruth that she was prepared to leave the god of her family, Chemosh, and trust in Yahweh, Naomi's God. Not even death was going to part the two women for Ruth declared that she would be buried where Naomi was buried.

This account shines with the priceless values of loyalty and friendship. Ruth had seen Naomi's faith in action and she herself was changed by the encounter. For Christians there is a choice we need to make. In the Gospel of John we read how Jesus chose the disciples and called them His friends, which took them beyond the relationship of Master and servant. The privilege of friendship with Jesus was to bring the disciples into conflict with worldly expectations. They were chosen to continue Jesus' teaching and, empowered by the Holy Spirit, became channels of God's inclusive love. "Choice" has a twin sister – "Consequence".

Discussion Starters

1. What choices have you made which have changed your life?

_____
_____
_____
_____

2. In Old Testament times, marriage was for companionship, to preserve the family tree as well as for children. There was also a certain amount of security for the wives so long as the husbands lived. Discuss the attitudes to marriage within different cultures today. Does this help us to understand Ruth's position?

_____
_____
_____
_____

3. In Moab, Mahlon and Chilion were the foreigners. Why does it seem to be easier for the men in a cross-cultural marriage?

_____
_____
_____
_____

4. Do you know anyone who has changed denomination or faith or country on marriage? How has it affected them?

_____
_____
_____
_____

5. Imagine how Ruth's family must have felt when she chose to go with Naomi to Bethlehem.

_____

_____

_____

_____

6. In what ways do you feel we have less close family bonds than in the days of Ruth?

_____

_____

_____

_____

7. Have you ever had the opportunity to witness for Jesus to someone of another faith?

_____

_____

_____

_____

8. What does it feel like to think of yourself as a _friend_ of Jesus?

_____

_____

_____

_____

Personal Application

Even in a multi-cultural setting, we still find ourselves mixing predominantly with our "own kind". The book of Ruth raises the profile of "the foreigner" by giving us the story of three women with whom we can identify. We see their hopes and fears and we journey with them as they make their choices alone. We also recognise that Naomi stood out for her unfaltering faith in a God who would protect her and whose divine providence would bring her ultimate shalom. It challenges our faith. God will guide us by the power of the Holy Spirit and the choices we need to make can be prayerfully committed to Him.

Seeing Jesus in the Scriptures

In the sorrowful parting of Naomi and Ruth from Orpah, we are reminded that Jesus, too, had close friends in Mary, Martha and Lazarus. Of the two occasions which record Jesus weeping, one is when Lazarus died. Our Lord Jesus needed the support and understanding of His friends and we, too, can thank God for those who share their friendship with us. Jesus made a point of telling His disciples that they had not chosen Him, but that He had chosen them. He also said that all who would be disciples must take up their cross and follow Him.

WEEK 3

New Beginnings

Opening Icebreaker

If you were to become a vegetable, which would you choose and why? For example, a broad bean is cocooned in a beautiful sleeping bag and also grows in a community with other beans ...

Bible Readings

- Ruth 1:19–22; 2:1–23
- Leviticus 19:9–10
- John 3:5–6
- Ephesians 4:22–24

Opening Our Eyes

Our story now begins the climb from despair to hope as Naomi and Ruth journey to Naomi's home in Bethlehem. It is with a heavy heart that poor old Naomi drags herself along the steep road from Moab and the Dead Sea, up through the Judean wilderness to the familiar terraced fields and olive groves of Bethlehem.

With the climate and fertility of the land, Bethlehem farmers could gather two harvests and the barley harvest meant that it was spring. So we gather the significance of these two widows arriving at a time of hope and new beginnings. Certainly, Naomi felt she was beginning all over again. As she says, she went away full and has returned empty. The ravages of bereavement and hardship on her face elicit shock and sympathy from her friends. For Ruth, this is a strange new land. She is suddenly a foreigner, an object of gossip and speculation.

So much is tantalisingly left unwritten. Was Naomi able to return to her original home? Were the two women given hospitality with friends or did they pitch their own tent? Whatever they did, they needed to eat and Ruth quickly takes the initiative to work with the harvesters. For Ruth and Naomi, the laws laid down in the book of Leviticus are a life-saver – or a God-send!

In any small community news spreads fast and in the little town of Bethlehem news had whistled around of Naomi's return. Not just that, but people had been amazed to learn how her Moabite daughter-in-law had embraced the faith of Israel. Everyone had heard – even the men.

Another story of how God used the faith of a girl in a foreign land is that of Naaman's little slave, as told in 2 Kings chapter 5. Time and time again throughout the Bible we meet great faith which surmounts all barriers of race and culture, age and gender. The God of Israel, the Holy One, is the God who offers new beginnings; the great and loving God honours the integrity and faithfulness of those who put their trust in Him.

Ruth begins the back-breaking work of gleaning, hardly resting for a moment and when Boaz comes along to see how things are progressing with the harvest, he immediately spots the new girl alongside his workers. For Boaz, this prominent Bethlehem farmer, wealthy but evidently unmarried, this meeting with the lovely young Moabite widow, proves to be a new beginning beyond his wildest dreams. Boaz offers her the protection of his girls, for he too has heard about Ruth's loyalty and kindness to her mother-in-law. However, from his remark that he had ordered his young men not to "bother" her, it is perfectly clear that a foreign girl was otherwise pitifully vulnerable.

We might pause to think also of the servants harvesting in the field. Perhaps it was a new experience for them to work with a Gentile.

Ruth has a new home, new friends and now a benefactor. Naomi, thrilled with Ruth's gleaning, declares Boaz to be one of her nearest relatives. Naomi immediately blesses the Lord for His providence, for her own security is directly tied to her daughter-in-law. To her, this change in their fortunes is the direct hand of God. Naomi hatches a plan ...

Discussion Starters

1. Have you ever been in the position of feeling like a "stranger" or a "foreigner"? In what situations have you had the opportunity to befriend a person who was a long way from their own home and familiar surroundings?

_____

_____

_____

_____

2. God's laws are directly for our own protection and wholeness. In what ways can you see problems when they are flouted?

_____

_____

_____

_____

3. Discuss an incident which could be described as a "God-send".

_____

_____

_____

_____

4. Is there a "new beginning" you would care to share with the group?

_____

_____

_____

_____

5. Ruth's reputation went before her. Discuss the importance of a good reputation and how does it differ to a Christian reputation?

_____

_____

_____

_____

6. Talk about the contemporary scandals regarding young girls being used as sex-slaves and for forced labour.

_____

_____

_____

_____

7. Naomi is totally dependent on Ruth. Think about family circumstances which affect different generations.

_____

_____

_____

_____

Personal Application

In Matthew chapter 7 verse 12, our Lord Jesus says, "So in everything, do to others what you would have them do to you, for this sums up the Law and the Prophets." As the story of Ruth unfolds we cannot but be touched by her genuine care and devotion to Naomi. Ruth is seen as exemplary in her relationships, honest, loyal, loving and God-fearing. What an example to us. As Christians we are called to be exemplary in our relationships, too, thus creating the climate and opportunities for others to be drawn to Jesus our Lord.

Seeing Jesus in the Scriptures

Our Lord Jesus said to Nicodemus that he needed to be born of the Spirit. We all need to make that new beginning in the Spirit. Such was Jesus' reputation that great crowds followed Him wherever He went. He drew close to those on the margins of society, speaking to a Samaritan woman, touching lepers and bringing the widow's son back to life. His whole ministry was of compassion and in His sacrifice upon the cross, heaven touched earth, God Himself broke into our human life.

WEEK 4

Loving Kindness/"*hesed*"

Opening Icebreaker

Continuing the vegetable theme from the last session, name a vegetable you dislike and will not eat. How hungry would you have to be before eating it? How different is our diet to that in Bethlehem in 800 BC?

Bible Readings

- Ruth 3:1–18
- Exodus 34:6
- Psalm 118:1
- Isaiah 63:7
- Titus 3:4

Opening Our Eyes

In this session we will unpack the key Hebrew word
hesed. One of the best ways to describe it is: God's
steadfast love towards His people within the covenant
relationship. Or, as David Atkinson puts it in *The Message
of Ruth*, "this merciful and gracious loving kindness ...".
It is that warm and loyal relationship as personified by
David and Jonathan and the long-suffering love shown
by God when the people rebel and run after other gods.

When Ruth vowed to stay with Naomi, to serve her God
and even to be buried where Naomi was buried, her
declaration was an act of *hesed*. She was showing loving
kindness beyond what was expected, literally Ruth was
prepared to go the extra mile. She was the epitome of
faithfulness and reliability; scarce attributes in those days
just as they are now. Exodus 34 verse 6 tells us that the
nature of God Himself is steadfast love and faithfulness
and for those who sought to be obedient to the God of
Israel, their faith and their moral life were inextricably
bound together. Perhaps we would say today, "faith in
action".

Certainly this is a core theme running through the book
of Ruth. It is implicit that Naomi showed loving kindness
to Ruth that Ruth, brought up to worship the god
Chemosh, should embrace the God of Israel. Ruth shows
hesed to Naomi's son, Chilion, until his early death and
then continues to care for her mother-in-law.

In chapter 2 we have already become aware of the
generosity and kindness with which Boaz has treated
Ruth, the outsider. Now, in this third chapter, we see
how one kind deed leads to another. Naomi praises the
providence of God in all this and dreams up a plan for
Ruth's, and her own, future security. In this plan she

herself is returning loving kindness towards her daughter-in-law. Naomi was inspired to set her sights on the inheritance for her late husband and son through her near relative, Boaz. Ruth, as a dutiful daughter-in-law, trusted that Naomi would always do the right thing and she obediently washed and perfumed herself before putting on her best clothes.

It was quite usual in biblical times for landowners to personally guard their crops, so Naomi would have been pretty certain that Boaz would spend the night at the threshing floor. The harvest was precious, for it literally meant the difference between life and death. The narrative is sensitive and tender as we follow Ruth to the threshing floor where Boaz had fallen into contented sleep. Some scholars of Hebrew feel that the word "feet" had a wider implication, and that Ruth was making a humble and sincere request for marriage. Rather than feeling himself compromised, Boaz seems overwhelmed that Ruth should look at him when there are many other, and younger, men around. He responds by promising to "do all that you ask", and in the morning, loads her with barley to take back home to Naomi. Gone now is Naomi's emptiness. The steadfast love of the Lord had not abandoned her after all.

We know extremely little about Boaz, but he is depicted as a man of honour. A man who greets his employees in the name of the Lord, and shows *hesed* to them and even to a foreign girl. He is a man whom the Lord God will use.

As the story races on, the writer uses the classic cliffhanger to end the chapter: "Wait, my daughter, until you find out what happens ..."

We too wait until the next session to follow God's providence.

Discussion Starters

1. Graham Kendrick has a truly inspirational gift of matching the Old and New Testaments for modern song. In one of his songs, "We are marching", the chorus is Psalm 118 verse 1 but the lead words from the verse are: "ever further and deeper into the heart of God". How do hymns, songs and choruses enrich your faith?

_____

_____

_____

_____

2. Over and over again, God's steadfast love is demonstrated to the recalcitrant people of Israel. How does this compare with Jesus' teaching on forgiveness – that we should forgive "seventy times seven"?

_____

_____

_____

_____

3. Share how, in your own experience, one kindness has led to another.

_____

_____

_____

_____

4. What would have been the practical reasons for Boaz to sleep at the threshing floor?

_____

_____

_____

_____

5. Compare Ruth's request to be covered by Boaz's garment to the way in which the Lord God of Israel "covers" His people.

_____

_____

_____

_____

6. Why do you think so many people today are embarrassed to talk about their faith?

_____

_____

_____

_____

7. Jesus said to one man whom He healed, "Go home to your family and tell them how much the Lord has done for you" (Mark 5:19). Testimonies have great impact – should we hear more of what God is doing in lives today?

_____

_____

_____

_____

Personal Application

This theme of loving kindness is one enormous challenge for Christians. Within the media, serious news or entertaining drama, the emphasis tilts heavily towards revenge. Everybody is encouraged to fight for their rights but little is articulated regarding responsibilities. Another great message in the book of Ruth is that of persistence and rewarded trust. How do we rate on the spiritual clapometer of perseverance and loving kindness?

Seeing Jesus in the Scriptures.

The entire recorded, short life of Jesus of Nazareth was one of loving kindness. We read He had compassion for the widow of Nain, that He was moved to compassion by the crowds and healed their sick – and in the greatest parable, Jesus spoke of the Samaritan taking pity on the man left for dead on the Jerusalem to Jericho road. His loving kindness even reached to the man who hung beside Him on the cross.

WEEK 5

Redemption

Opening Icebreaker

There are very few words which are instantly recognisable in most languages. Spend a few minutes deciding what these words might be. The leader has the three most popular answers, but you may find others.

Bible Readings

- Ruth 4:1–12
- Deuteronomy 25:5–10
- Job 19:25
- Isaiah 41:14
- Colossians 1:13–14;
- 1 Peter 1:18–19

Opening Our Eyes

Travelling in the coach after visiting the Garden of Gethsemane, our group began singing the song: "There is a Redeemer, Jesus, God's own Son". I never sing those words now without being taken back in time and remembering our corporate gratitude for what God had done for each one of us.

In this fourth chapter of Ruth, we follow the working out of two ancient Israelite customs. First, the *levirate* marriage and secondly – this being fundamental to the understanding of God's covenant relationship with His people – the *goel*.

Levir is the Latin word used to translate the Hebrew for brother-in-law and a levirate marriage was the accepted custom of keeping the family together. In our very individualistic society, we miss a great deal of the significance of these biblical customs because they evolved to consolidate and protect the family group and the community as a whole. When a man died childless, he appeared to have died completely. If his brother then married and had a son by the widow, then that son was deemed to be the heir of the dead man, thus the deceased's "name" would live on to strengthen the family members and the family possessions which, in other words, meant land.

So we begin to grasp the importance of the *levir* in those times. In the third chapter of Ruth, we have seen how Ruth makes her request for marriage to the "near relative", Boaz. Now, as we enter into chapter 4, we come across the man who is a closer relative than Boaz and therefore has first entitlement to Ruth.

Cleverly, Boaz offers the man the land first before telling him that he would, of course, have to marry Ruth as well!

For his own reasons the man, while accepting the land, could not accept the Moabite widow. The way was then clear for Boaz and, by taking Ruth in a levirate marriage, Boaz also becomes the *goel*, the kinsman-redeemer.

The concept of the *goel or* kinsman-redeemer highlights a mega-theme throughout the Word of God, that of redemption. Looking into the early laws enshrined in Leviticus (25:25–28, 47–54), we see that the act of redemption was to purchase a slave back to freedom. It is clear that the redeemer was vital to the restoration of the poor. If there was no kinsman, then the king became the person to whom the slave turned. If this failed then over and above earthly kings was the Lord God of Israel Himself. We read how Naomi says that she had gone away full only to return empty. She had gone to Moab a wife and mother, but returned a widow, at the mercy of a kinsman-redeemer. In the language of deliverance, the words redemption and salvation are closely interlinked.

Throughout the Old Testament we trace the theme of Israel's God, Yahweh, redeeming His people. First, by bringing them out of bondage in Egypt, then through prophets like Isaiah and Jeremiah, the Holy One of Israel is called "your Redeemer". Out of exile and oppression, God redeemed the people with that overwhelming steadfast love and mercy, that *hesed* for His chosen people. However, the implications of the word *goel* reach further than kindness and family obligation; the implications move into the realms of cost and payment.

Jesus Christ, God's Son, is *our* Redeemer. From the poverty of our sin, we have been bought back into the family of God through His sacrifice on the cross. Jesus paid the price of our sin that we might know forgiveness and reconciliation and enter into the freedom of eternal life.

Discussion Starters

1. Does the contemporary idea of "godparent" bear any relation to the ancient custom of the kinsman-redeemer?

_____

_____

_____

_____

2. What, do you imagine, could have been the reasons why the nearest kinsman-redeemer refused to marry Ruth?

_____

_____

_____

_____

3. It is interesting that Boaz mentions "the town records" and we realise the importance of the family tree in biblical times. Think about how famous Boaz was to become in those same town records.

_____

_____

_____

_____

4. Deuteronomy and Leviticus contained laws which placed great obligation upon the "haves" to assist the "have-nots". They also contain the law governing the Year of Jubilee. How does this fit in with our attitudes to the Third World debt?

_____

_____

_____

_____

5. The sublime statement by Job (19:25) highlights the very personal nature of the Redeemer. At his lowest point, Job clings onto his faith. Have you been able to hold onto your faith in difficult situations?

_____

_____

_____

_____

6. Jesus Christ "redeemed" us by His death at Calvary. Have you ever paused to think of the cost to God's Son of such a death and how does your response square with the price He paid?

_____

_____

_____

_____

7. Redemption for the Christian leads to reconciliation (Rom. 5:10) and reconciliation leads to peace (Eph. 2:16–17). Think about this role of the Christian in family, work, leisure, the community as a whole.

_____

_____

_____

_____

Personal application

The belief that Jesus died for our sins is crucial to our Christian faith. Nearly everyone would have to say that Jesus lived and Jesus died. His life was documented by others outside the disciples' group, He was a figure of history; but not everyone can say *why* He died. To accept Jesus as our Redeemer is to turn from the attitudes and values of the world and throw ourselves upon the mercy of His everlasting loving kindness.

Seeing Jesus in the Scriptures

One of the great verses of the New Testament is Revelation chapter 5 verse 9. This portrays Jesus as God's Messiah, the Redeemer of the world. Jesus, the First and the Last, at God's right hand for eternity. This is none other than the saving power of God.

WEEK 6

Witnesses

Opening Icebreaker

Everyone have a go at miming a book or film that you have recently enjoyed. If the mime is not guessed, then simply tell the others about it!

Bible Readings

- Ruth 4:9–21
- 1 Samuel 12:5
- Isaiah 43:10
- Acts 1:8
- 1 John 1:2–4

Opening Our Eyes

In the marriage service, the couple have to make legal declarations. In front of witnesses they have to say: "I call upon these persons here present, to witness that I ... take thee ... to be my lawful wedded wife/husband." When a will is prepared, it has to be signed by two witnesses. Perhaps we are more familiar with the television dramas in which people are called to stand in the witness box. Even though this story is around 3,000 years old, we have no trouble at all with the concept of witness.

As the story of Ruth comes to its conclusion we are able to discern the value of witnessing – in this particular tale, throughout both the Old and the New Testaments and our own, present-day witness. From the outset, Naomi must have been a shining witness to her faith. In her words, prayers and actions, it became obvious to Ruth that Yahweh, the God of the Israelites, was a God to be trusted. Even when her husband and then her two sons died, Naomi continued to look to her God for guidance and protection. This made such an enormous impact on the young Ruth, that she turned her back on the god of the Moabites to embrace Judaism.

The second chapter shows just how much notice people were taking of Ruth. They witnessed her hard work (2:7) and also heard the whispers of how kind she had been to her husband and mother-in-law (2:11).

Boaz, too, was a man with a reputation for justice and kindness. He offered the young foreign worker the protection of his own girl servants, he shared his bread and wine with her and told the men servants to be extra generous (2:15–16). His servants were all able to witness his generosity in his dealings with the vulnerable in daily life. A testimony indeed to this wealthy man.

In the fourth chapter, the scene is set at the city gate. Boaz is waiting for the nearest relative of Naomi to pass by. He also called ten elders of the city to witness the proposed transactions. The city gate was a good place in ancient times to strike deals and, even today, the Damascus Gate in Jerusalem offers a glimpse of how things might have looked. All the traders, the bustle, the women with jars on their heads, the donkeys bringing their burdens into the city, the colours of the fruit, the general noise and pulse of life.

Boaz gives an elated short speech (4:9–10) in which he tells the world that he has acquired all that had belonged to Elimelech, Chilion and Mahlon, as well as Ruth the Moabitess so that the dead men's names may live on. By the response, we realise that heaps of people had stopped to watch what was going on – "… *all* those at the gate said, 'We are witnesses …'" (italics mine).

More than this, when Ruth and Boaz had their first baby son, Obed, the women gathered round as Naomi took the boy on her lap. They witnessed the tender love of a grandmother whose life had been redeemed. Obed would now be her pride and joy into old age.

The New Testament also has witnesses. Most notably, Jesus speaks to His disciples and tells them that they will be witnesses to Him not only in Jerusalem, Judea and Samaria, but to the whole world. What a challenge! What a responsibility for present-day disciples – to be witnesses for the Lord Jesus Christ. Boaz and Ruth take their place in the family tree of both King David and our Lord and Saviour Jesus Christ. Out of the pages of ancient Scripture their lives are paragons of kindness and faith, challenging us in our time and place to trust in God's guidance, providence and redeeming love.

Discussion Starters

1. It's so easy to notice things when they are not done and people are quick to spot bad behaviour. Are we so quick to appreciate work and kind behaviour? In what ways can we be affirming?

_____

_____

_____

_____

2. Anybody in public life is under constant scrutiny. Discuss how you would cope if you had media attention on your own life.

_____

_____

_____

_____

3. Why do you think people outside the Church are so interested in scandals affecting Christians? Is it unreasonable to expect higher standards from Christians?

_____

_____

_____

_____

4. If people were talking about you, how would you hope that they would describe you?

_____

_____

_____

_____

5. Have you any recollections of grandparents' faith or older members of your church who encouraged your own journey?

_____
_____
_____
_____

6. The apostle John was definite in all that had been "seen and heard". He witnessed to the saving power of the Lord Jesus Christ during the early days of the Christian communities. How do you see the impact of "testimony" today?

_____
_____
_____
_____

7. Imagine you were a first-century Christian. Thinking of Acts 4:31–37, in what ways would your witness differ from today?

_____
_____
_____
_____

8. How do you answer the jibe that, for a lot of the population, there would be insufficient evidence to convict them of being Christian?

_____
_____
_____
_____

9. How can we be witnesses without putting people off?

_____
_____
_____
_____

Personal Application

It is so important to live out our faith in daily life. Christianity is not a Sunday mask but the outworking of Christ's love in our attitudes and actions – especially when life goes pear-shaped. The apostle James wrote that "faith without deeds is dead". Again, the echo of morality and spirituality intertwined. It is hard work. It takes *all* the fruit of the Spirit (Gal. 5:22).

Seeing Jesus in the Scriptures

The crowds witnessed Jesus in His teaching and healing, in His attitude towards the lowly and those on the margins of society. They watched and listened and talked about Him (Mark 8:28). They marvelled at His authority and at the miracles He performed and they flocked in such numbers that it was sometimes hard for Jesus to get any peace. His reputation was such that even Pontius Pilate's wife had heard about Him and, try as he might, Pilate couldn't lay any crime on Jesus. Five hundred people witnessed His resurrection appearances. Jesus lived the perfect life and the New Testament bears witness to the fact of His life, death and resurrection.

WEEK 7

Lineage of David

Opening Icebreaker

Now that you are familiar with the characters in the book of Ruth, say which person, named or unnamed, you best identify with and/or which you would enjoy playing in a film about Ruth.

Bible Readings

- Ruth 4:13–22
- 1 Samuel 16:4–13
- Micah 5:2
- Luke 2:1–7
- John 7:40–42

Opening Our Eyes

To our twenty-first-century ears, the conclusion to this book is delightful. Ruth and Boaz are proud parents of a bouncing baby boy and dear old Naomi takes on a new lease of life with a beloved grandson to whom she can tell her wealth of stories. We can almost hear music fading away as we close the book. However, to the ears of people living six, seven or eight hundred years BC, the closing words of Ruth are a positive bombshell!

We have already touched upon how the prophet Ezra viewed a "mixed" marriage and yet here was Ruth, the foreign girl from Moab, becoming the great-grandmother of Israel's second king, David. It was unthinkable! A scandal!

The message in this Spirit-inspired book of Holy Scripture is loud and clear. Faithfulness, loyalty and loving kindness are more important to our Father God than the purity of the Israelite blood-line. After all, God created all people. Those who offer themselves in humble obedience and trust His divine providence are the men and women through whom His purposes and love will be made known. That was true for the time of Ruth and it is equally true for us some 3,000 years later.

By the time the book of Ruth was written, David was the heroic king. His name stood amongst the great men of God – Abraham, Moses … David. David achieved almost cult status, the mighty warrior, the charismatic leader whose treasured psalms are still loved. Now the people had evidence that this exalted King David had foreign blood in his veins.

When the prophet Micah, the contemporary of Isaiah and Hosea, spoke to the people of Israel, he shockingly predicted the end of their kings. Yet the focus of Micah's hopes lie in the coming of God's Messiah. This Messiah would be born in Bethlehem and "his greatness will reach to the ends of the earth. And he will be their peace" (Micah 5:4–5).

What a wonderful revelation that Ruth is a direct ancestor of Jesus Christ Himself, who was born in Bethlehem, because Joseph was of the house and lineage of David. Our God is so incredible. Despite all the difficulties and tragedies which we see with our limited human sight, God's purposes and His timing are perfect.

Jesus, the Messiah, born in the little town of Bethlehem, "the house of bread", was to say to His disciples, "I am the bread of life" (John 6:35). The way in which the story of Naomi and Ruth moves from emptiness to new life and hope is the journey each of us make from our self-centred, empty lives to life in all its fullness (John 10:10). By the power of the Holy Spirit we are born again to new life in Jesus, our Messiah.

In the perplexing, dramatic and fascinating book of Revelation, we meet the new kingdom. In the wake of destruction and despair there is the profound promise that God will be with His people and in chapter 22 verse 16 we read: "I, Jesus, have sent my angel to give you this testimony for the churches. I am the Root and the Offspring of David ..."

Discussion Starters

1. In our culture of "grasp and greed", there are always those men and women whose Christian ideals inspire others. Discuss a local or national "name" whose Christian principles are a shining witness.

_____

_____

_____

_____

2. Thinking about Jesus' ancestry, how do you interpret His teachings towards those on the margins of society?

_____

_____

_____

_____

3. Is there a particular psalm which you think would have made an impression on Jesus as He learned at the feet of the teachers of the law?

_____

_____

_____

_____

4. Write down something of your experience of new life in Christ. Perhaps you might like to share this.

_____

_____

_____

_____

5. A grandmother's influence can be immense. Naomi looked after the young Obed and would have forged strong bonds with the boy. How important are these family influences on our coming to faith?

_____

_____

_____

_____

6. The book of Ruth is read in synagogues at the festival of Shavuot, which falls seven weeks after the Passover. Do you think our standard of living lessens the impact of such festivals ?

_____

_____

_____

_____

7. The prophet projected the Messiah as the Prince of Peace, a ruler of justice and compassion, one whose kingdom would never end. How do we reconcile the coming of Jesus with the world in the state it is in today?

_____

_____

_____

_____

Personal Application

We need to take to heart the sayings: "It's not *what* you are but *who* you are that counts" and "People don't care how much you know so long as they know how much you care". The example of the characters within the story of Ruth demonstrate that kindness is contagious. These are all ordinary, meek people with no position to flout but, as the apostle Paul wrote, God uses the weak to confound the mighty and in our weakness we are made strong in the Lord.

Seeing Jesus in the Scriptures

By the end of the book of Ruth we see clearly how the story is part of the Jesus story. This is His background, His people, the family tree into which He was born in Bethlehem. The spectacularly precise prophecies in the Old Testament leave us awed by God's hand in human history. And human history is our history. Jesus Christ, God's Son, is our Messiah, our Redeemer, who in mystery and miracle lives in the Spirit to work through us His love and compassion in a bleak world. Ultimately, the victory is secured – His kingdom has no end.

Leader's Notes

Week 1: Disaster

Icebreaker

Some groups may know each other well; on the other hand, this may be the first meeting for some. Over the next weeks the quality of your sharing will deepen if there is trust and understanding between the group members. It can be quite fascinating to use a world map and it will be used next week as well, so keep the pins in situ for the recap.

Bible Readings

The key reading is Ruth while the other readings offer background to the context for the story. The verses reinforce the teachings of the Lord God through Moses as well as the Israelites' prejudices. It may be a helpful practice to insert bookmarks into the relevant pages so that you are not fumbling around in possibly unfamiliar Bible territory.

Aim of the Session

In this first week it is important to get over the message that this is not just a nice little tale of country folk slotted in somewhere as an ideal of family virtues. Any study of the Bible is layered and leaves us with many tangent questions and the book of Ruth is no different. Here in the very first verse there is a conundrum. Bethlehem was the last place to expect famine and Moab was absolutely the last place for an Israelite family to look for a new life. By the end of the fifth verse the family has been whammed into tragedy. Draw out how many circumstances experienced by people today appear totally unfair and devastating. The geographical, political and social context of the story makes Ruth's "conversion" all the more wonderful. Explore the influence of Naomi's faith and look at the challenge that makes to us in our families. Register in the mind of the group the total trust in God's providence shown by both Naomi and Ruth.

Week 2: Choices

Icebreaker

To follow a world map theme for the second time will
bring back things from last week and generally help
people feel relaxed in an informal atmosphere. It should
be clear that it is God's world and, as part of His creation,
none of us lives in isolation. The miracles of
communication bring the world far closer than previous
generations could have ever envisaged and we are
blessed with the opportunities of travel.

Aim of the Session

You could contrast the travelling that Elimelech's family
experienced – *walking* into a new country with all their
possessions – with the media pictures of refugees today.
Whilst millions of people desperately seek a new life,
others jet around the world with ease.

The Bible readings are all about choices and there are
other portions of Scripture involving choice which could
be mentioned: Rebekah choosing to deceive Isaac; the
people of Jerusalem shouting their choice of Barabas ...
etc.

However, this portion of the book of Ruth shows how
Naomi prayerfully put all her trust and confidence in her
God. She recognised the total powerlessness of her
bereaved situation and surrendered to God's providence.
She did not understand, she had no idea what was to
become of her, but God was her strength in time of
greatest grief and anxiety. God was such an ever-present
reality to Naomi that she was an unconscious evangelist.

Draw out the fact that Ruth already believed in Chemosh.
It is often easier to come to faith when a person has not

had a previous faith, than to leave one faith behind for another. Most people receive a belief by the accident of their birthplace. Naomi must have been a remarkable woman and it was a wonderful testimony to her that Ruth chose to follow the God of Israel.

You can bring these characters to life in a refreshing way for the group. Naomi had chosen to return to Bethlehem, but she believed the girls should remain in their own land. Here is a struggle with custom and need, devotion and selflessness. They are not merely names from dry old history, but real people, with real problems to deal with and real choices to figure out – with no one to help them but God.

Just look at Naomi's prayer: "May the Lord show kindness to you" (vv.8–9). True prayer is when our own desires come secondary to the needs of those we love.

Key sentence: "Your people will be my people and your God my God" (v.16). Ruth had made her momentous choice.

Week 3: New Beginnings

Icebreaker

Now that the group are feeling more comfortable with
each other, they can indulge in flights of fancy and have
fun with this one. It may be necessary to begin in a
lighter vein for, quite possibly, one or more of the group
may have difficult associations with this session's title.

Aim of the Session

The Leviticus reading highlights the moral code of the
law. Today the agricultural policy is for extracting the last
grain for profit, there are no sheaves left behind – even
for Harvest Festival displays! There is a more serious side
to this in that in the British Isles there is a serious decline
in wildlife as a direct consequence of over-farming.
Consider the fallow year and the set-aside policy. God's
law allows people, animals and land to live in harmony.
The other readings concern the new beginnings. Being
"born again", becoming a "new creation" in Jesus Christ.
Too often we try to bend God's laws to suit ourselves
whereas Jesus confronted this ploy by teaching that new
wine could not be stored in old wineskins.

We all identify with new beginnings. Each new day is a
new beginning. In fact, every breath we take is a new
breath and each moment of the day leads us into
uncharted waters – we tend to think of new beginnings in
dramatic terms only. The lives of Ruth, Naomi and Boaz
reflect lives around us today where bereavement,
redundancy, accident, crime or birth, all bring about a
new, often daunting and unfamiliar phase. There are
some occasions when we underestimate the trauma of a
new way of life, such as when a son or daughter has left
home. Outsiders may be saying, "Well done", "What a
good move" and so on, while the parents suddenly face

an empty place at the table and a *tidy* hall devoid of football boots and draped sweatshirts. New beginnings need a certain amount of adjustment and understanding. We thank God that He begins each breath, each step, with us.

Week 4: Loving Kindness/"*hesed*"

Icebreaker
This is to bring out the fact of our overwhelming choice –
and that the more choice we have the more fussy we
tend to become. Parents and grandparents did not have
such choice and they would be shocked at current
levels of waste. We are blessed with "plenty" and our
comfortable position should alert us to greater
responsibility to food resources. In a light-hearted way
a serious point is able to be made.

Aim of the Session
Try to look at all the Bible readings which give examples
of God's loving kindness; "*hesed*" is His divine essence
and nature. Our own language can be somewhat narrow
and so the group's appreciation of the great Hebrew word
needs to be broadened. It is similar in its breadth of
meaning to the way in which shalom means so much
more than simply "peace". Think of the rich overtones
of God's attitude towards us and our pale response to
His love.

This covertly racy chapter is not the portion usually read
in morning worship! If we hadn't been captivated by
Naomi's deep faith – and loving kindness – in the
previous chapters, it could almost appear that she was
behaving like a wanton schemer. However, the story
unfolds to reveal the character of Boaz. He does not take
advantage of Ruth, rather he is amazed that she should
bother with him when there were so many other younger
men available. Boaz understands completely that Ruth is
offering herself in marriage and he is concerned that she
should not be seen there with him. His generosity is
shown in his concern for her reputation and also in the
six measures of barley which Ruth takes home, like a
prize, to her mother-in-law.

This key word is the link between all the characters in this story reflecting the nature of God's relationship with His people. It also gives an indication of the harmony and reward of life lived in loving kindness. Link these with the teaching of Jesus in the Sermon on the Mount (Matt. 5). You may also like to refer to Romans 12 verses 9–18. If we seek to live in a right relationship with our God then our lives must be bathed in prayer for this "*hesed*", for it is the lifestyle of Jesus our Lord.

Week 5: Redemption

Icebreaker
Three of the most common words that have international recognition are: OK, Coke and Hallelujah. There are bound to be some good suggestions from the group. Language can divide as well as unite and being unable to communicate can be a harrowing experience.

Aim of the Session
The Bible readings follow this theological ribbon of redemption that binds the Old and New Testaments together. It is also an interesting peep into the social customs, laws and conventions of biblical times as the people of Israel established themselves from nomadic tribes into a community and a nation. Jeremiah acted as a kinsman-redeemer for his cousin Hanamel (Jer. 32). The family name was paramount and, at all costs, the heirs and inheritance had to be safeguarded.

Nothing in the Bible is without significance. The living echoes from one generation to another speak to us not only of the past but also of our own involvement as heirs of Christ. Through Him we have been "redeemed", we have "salvation". This last, rather old-fashioned word, has its roots in the word *salve* – which is all bound up with the meaning of health and wholeness, the shalom or peace of God.

Through the characters in this story, we are able to reflect on the features of redemption working in the death and resurrection of our Lord Jesus Christ (See Eph. 1:7.) When we drink the wine at the Eucharist, the Holy Communion or the Lord's Supper, we partake the symbol of the blood of the new covenant. Christ is our *goel*, our kinsman-Redeemer. The enormity of this fact cannot be digested without an experience of faith.

Week 6: Witnesses

Icebreaker

Films and books are but a twenty-first-century version of sitting around the campfire, listening to stories such as Ruth. We can learn some very valuable lessons from contemporary fiction, "faction", real-life drama or biography. There was an old Victorian hymn which began: "God has given us a book full of stories ..." and it is wonderful to see the resurgence of "story" in many aspects of life from faith to therapy.

Aim of the Session

It may be very uncomfortable to people within the group to come to terms with the fact that Christians are, for many, a curiosity and, for some, even a joke. The media never tires of portraying church and those involved with it as wimps, sly or just pathetic. Explain how in the story of Ruth the characters are all strongly portrayed. Ruth would never have been prompted to leave her god Chemosh by a pathetic, colourless little lady from Bethlehem.

After the resurrection and Pentecost, the disciples suddenly went into the world with courage and a mission. They told the life and death of Jesus, as they had witnessed it, with clarity and passion.

Any witness who shillyshallies in a court of law is torn to shreds by the barristers. But if we know a thing to be true, then there is no hesitation, no questioning in our minds – we can speak and act accordingly and people will notice.

Encourage the group to see that whatever we do or say is heard and seen by somebody. As the folk in Bethlehem watched Ruth and judged her, so we are judged by the way we behave. This is not just a story from the past, it shows us how we are witnesses for our Lord in our time and place.

Week 7: Lineage of David

Icebreaker

At the end of these sessions people may have some interesting things to say about which character they would like to be in a film. Encourage the group to value the character chosen. You may end up with four Ruths, but more poignant would be to have an Orpah. It would also be interesting to notice which character is avoided.

Aim of the Session

The Bible readings focus on the references to Bethlehem. It was regarded as quite an insignificant place in comparison to Jerusalem only six miles away. Yet Bethlehem has a pivotal place within God's purposes.

Perhaps you are now encountering the *real* reason why this book was written in the first place. Our gracious and almighty God breaks into our human history to prepare the way for His anointed, the Messiah, the Saviour of the world. His ancestry must be approved, reaching back to Abraham in Matthew's Gospel and to Adam in Luke's Gospel. And Matthew, the Gospel writer so fond of scriptural references, even names Ruth in the genealogy, which for a patriachal setting speaks volumes for the veneration of Ruth.

You can remind the group of the vital importance of the family line in biblical times. In the book of Ruth we meet people who fear the Lord and obey His commands. We engage with them as disaster strikes and we watch the hand of God guide them as they begin all over again. They speak to us of commitment, loyalty, fidelity, loving kindness and trust in Israel's God. Remind the group that this is OUR God, too. Sometimes we get so carried away looking at how God has acted at a particular time, that we forget He is working out His purposes here and now!

So the book closes with the disclosure that Ruth is the great-grandmother to Israel's second king, David, and therefore a direct ancestor of Jesus of Nazareth – who was born in Bethlehem.

The alien and the widow have been brought from the bottom of the social pile into the genealogy of the Messiah. Not only is this the line of David, but it throws into sharp relief the nature of God's kingdom where those who mourn will be comforted, where the meek will inherit the earth and the merciful will be shown mercy. The great echoes of Scripture ripple out of the brief chapters of Ruth to engage us with the Living Word. Challenge the group to see that the story was written for us!

National Distributors

UK: (and countries not listed below)
CWR, Waverley Abbey House, Waverley Lane, Farnham, Surrey GU9 8EP.
Tel: (01252) 784710 Outside UK (44) 1252 784710

AUSTRALIA: CMC Australasia, PO Box 519, Belmont, Victoria 3216.
Tel: (03) 5241 3288

CANADA: CMC Distribution Ltd, PO Box 7000, Niagara on the Lake, Ontario L0S 1JO.
Tel: 1800 325 1297

GHANA: Challenge Enterprises of Ghana, PO Box 5723, Accra.
Tel: (021) 222437/223249 Fax: (021) 226227

HONG KONG: Cross Communications Ltd, 1/F, 562A Nathan Road, Kowloon.
Tel: 2780 1188 Fax: 2770 6229

INDIA: Crystal Communications, 10-3-18/4/1, East Marredpally, Secunderabad – 500 026.
Tel/Fax: (040) 7732801

KENYA: Keswick Bookshop, PO Box 10242, Nairobi.
Tel: (02) 331692/226047 Fax: (02) 728557

MALAYSIA: Salvation Book Centre (M) Sdn Bhd, 23 Jalan SS 2/64,
47300 Petaling Jaya, Selangor.
Tel: (03) 78766411/78766797 Fax: (03) 78757066/78756360

NEW ZEALAND: CMC Australasia, PO Box 36015, Lower Hutt.
Tel: 0800 449 408 Fax: 0800 449 049

NIGERIA: FBFM, Helen Baugh House, 96 St Finbarr's College Road, Akoka, Lagos.
Tel: (01) 7747429/4700218/825775/827264

PHILIPPINES: OMF Literature Inc, 776 Boni Avenue, Mandaluyong City.
Tel: (02) 531 2183 Fax: (02) 531 1960

REPUBLIC OF IRELAND: Scripture Union, 40 Talbot Street, Dublin 1.
Tel: (01) 8363764

SINGAPORE: Armour Publishing Pte Ltd, Block 203A Henderson Road,
11–06 Henderson Industrial Park, Singapore 159546.
Tel: 276 9976 Fax: 276 7564

SOUTH AFRICA: Struik Christian Books, 80 MacKenzie Street,
PO Box 1144, Cape Town 8000.
Tel: (021) 462 4360 Fax: (021) 461 3612

SRI LANKA: Christombu Books, 27 Hospital Street, Colombo 1.
Tel: (01) 433142/328909

TANZANIA: CLC Christian Book Centre, PO Box 1384, Mkwepu Street, Dar es Salaam.
Tel/Fax: (022) 2119439

USA: CMC Distribution, PO Box 644, Lewiston, New York, 14092-0644.
Tel: 1800 325 1297

ZIMBABWE: Word of Life Books, Shop 4, Memorial Building,
35 S Machel Avenue, Harare.
Tel: (04) 781305 Fax: (04) 774739

For email addresses, visit the CWR website: www.cwr.org.uk

Cover to Cover
Bible Study Guides

These exciting new study guides from the *Cover to Cover* range have been created to provide a unique resource for group and individual study sessions lasting between one and two hours.

The seven stimulating sessions in each title include opening icebreakers, Bible references, discussion starters and suggestions for personal application. There is an introduction that sets the topic in context as well as helpful notes for group leaders.

The Image of God
His Attributes and Character
ISBN: 1-85345-228-9

The Tabernacle
Entering into God's Presence
ISBN: 1-85345-230-0

The Uniqueness of our Faith
What makes Christianity Distinctive?
ISBN: 1-85345-232-7

Ruth
Loving Kindness in Action
ISBN: 1-85345-231-9

Mark
Life as it is Meant to be Lived
ISBN: 1-85345-233-5

Ephesians
Claiming your Inheritance
ISBN: 1-85345-229-7

£3.49 each